THE ECLIPSES

Poems by
DAVID WOO

○ ○ ○

A. POULIN, JR. NEW POETS OF AMERICA SERIES, NO. 27

BOA Editions, Ltd. ○ Rochester, NY ○ 2005

First Edition
05 06 07 08   7 6 5 4 3 2 1

Publications by BOA Editions, Ltd.—a not-for-profit corporation
under section 501 C (3) of the United States Internal Revenue Code—
are made possible with the assistance of grants from
the Literature Program of the New York State Council on the Arts;
the Literature Program of the National Endowment for the Arts;
the Sonia Raiziss Giop Charitable Foundation; the Lannan Foundation;
the Mary S. Mulligan Charitable Trust; the County of Monroe, NY;
the Rochester Area Community Foundation; the Elizabeth F. Cheney Foundation;
the Ames-Amzalak Memorial Trust in memory of
Henry Ames, Semon Amzalak and Dan Amzalak;
the Chadwick-Loher Foundation in honor of Charles Simic and Ray Gonzalez;
the Steeple-Jack Fund; and the CIRE Foundation,
as well as contributions from many individuals nationwide.

See Colophon on page 80 for special individual acknowledgments.

Cover Design: Geri McCormick
Cover Art: "Rotating Lamp" by David Woo
Interior Design and Composition: Richard Foerster
Manufacturing: McNaughton & Gunn, Lithographers
BOA Logo: Mirko

Library of Congress Cataloging-in-Publication Data

Woo, David, 1959-
The eclipses : poems / by David Woo.— 1st ed.
    p. cm. — (A. Poulin, Jr. new poets of America series ; no. 27)
ISBN 1–929918–61–5 (pbk. : alk. paper)
I. Title. II. Series: A. Poulin, Jr. new poets of America series ; v. 27.

PS3623.O6E27 2005
811'.6--dc22

2005001150

NATIONAL
ENDOWMENT
FOR THE ARTS

BOA Editions, Ltd.
Thom Ward, Editor
David Oliveiri, Chair
A. Poulin, Jr., President & Founder (1938–1996)
260 East Avenue, Rochester, NY 14604
www.boaeditions.org

State of the Arts

NYSCA

To my father and in memory of my mother

*You mustn't forget how many years your father and mother have lived,
as an occasion for pleasure and disquiet.*

—Confucius

I

Eden

Yellow-oatmeal flowers of the windmill palms
like brains lashed to fans—
even they think of cool paradise,

not this sterile air-conditioned chill
or the Arizona hell in which they sway becomingly.
Every time I return to Phoenix I see these palms

as a child's height marks on a kitchen wall,
taller now than the yuccas they were planted with,
taller than the Texas sage trimmed

to a perfect gray-green globe with pointillist
lavender blooms, taller than I,
who stopped growing years ago and commenced instead

my slow, almost imperceptible slouch
to my parents' old age:
Father's painful bend—really a bending of a bend—

to pick up the paper at the end of the sidewalk;
Mother, just released from Good Samaritan,
curled sideways on a sofa watching the soaps,

an unwanted tear inching down
at the plight of some hapless Hilary or Tiffany.
How she'd rail against television as a waste of time!

Now, with one arthritis-mangled hand,
she aims the remote control at the set
and flicks it off in triumph, turning to me

as I turn to the trees framed in the Arcadia door.
Her smile of affection melts into the back of my head,
a throb that presses me forward,

hand pressed to glass. I feel the desert heat
and see the beautiful shudders of the palms in the yard
and wonder why I despised this place so,

why I moved from city to temperate city, anywhere
without palms and cactus trees.
I found no paradise, as my parents know,

but neither did they, with their eager sprinklers
and scrawny desert plants pumped up to artificial splendor,
and their lives sighing away, exhaling slowly,

the man and woman
who teach me now as they could not before
to prefer real hell to any imaginary paradise.

The Repetitions

When he kneels in the gravel
to wire the wayward ocotillo to the post,
he twists his head sideways, as through
a proffered torque, then lets his torso follow
a beat or two behind, in the same, curious way
Father clips a corner hedge
or inspects a juniper, hammer hanging
from the same loop, right, oblique,
on the same brand of tool belt.

Vision corrected to something like
perfect, she still swerves the car to the right
when we gossip heatedly, as we tend to do,
about Aunt K.'s latest disaster or Cousin L.'s
disastrous marriage, just as Mother,
when she could drive, used to lurch
the old Bonneville toward the telephone poles
till we cried, "Telephone pole!"—and she,
serenely, shruggingly, averted disaster.

The three of us wait among pots of prickly pear
opposite the low partition of the nurse's
station. My sister plops in her seat,
muttering about the doctor, Slavic-surnamed,
who's "definitely not in the Chekhov mode."
My brother, the quiet one, sits with his arms
held tight within the armrests of his chair,
skimming a magazine with a trout on its cover.
Jet-lagged, I pace before a round window
like a porthole, glancing at a mirage I see
on the desert streets below, the same unreal water
I used to chase as a child. "Three children

from three different lanes of the gene pool,"
our mother once described us, affectionately,
but when the P.A. plays a Muzak version
of "King of the Road," one of her favorites,
we turn to each other and smile the same smile:
helpless, self-conscious, slightly lopsided,
like our father's.

My Father at 21

"My innocence back then was real, not a style,"
"a green flame of water as the bomber attacked"—
gnomic utterances, Heraclitean fragments:
I step through the evidence of you, like dust motes.

The swarming dust-cloud that hovered on the edge
of the green sea, you a single mote stepping into
the argent hull of a Pan Am prop plane,
the VIP lounge closed to you on the other end.

I have the photograph: you on a San Francisco street—
Geary or Sutter—in an oversized bomber jacket,
strolling toward the basement where thirty years later
I sipped coffee and read *The Way of Chuang Tz'u.*

That leanness, that angular intensity, so readily confused
with vacuity or boredom: the mouth empty
of words, save those gleaned from a dog-eared
pocket dictionary, each word nervously earned.

Inside the lining of the jacket a ganglion of nerves
firing each time a beautiful face enters
the peripheries, and then that sheepish blur,
our common diffidence, my inheritance.

Or smiling in wonder, the same tremble at the corners
of our lips, as on the long concourse you searched
for a face that matched the photographs
and, a grown man, saw your own father the first time.

Grandfather's Rockery

The verge bore the remnants of his shearings,
green splinters on red gravel, where he knelt
to the earth to sight his plane of grass:
flat as he could make it. And the blooms—

pink-veined sorrels, star-petaled, yellow glaring
bracts—made a long, scraggly S alongside,
to "undo the symmetry," he said, marking for us
his own boundary between order and chaos.

Oh, he believed in repression: his shears
cutting the uneven cowlicks of grass,
shaping his flowers to the desired asymmetry—
even in chaos a delineation. And the jagged

lines of his rockery—Guilin's peaks reduced
to the crude essence of karst edges—struggled
to hold back, scale back, the imposing presence
of remembered mountains. Their majesty, too,

was miniaturized like a transistor or microchip,
so that we would peer into the stone hollows,
the tiny carp lake, and see nothing, splendors
too subtle to perceive. Only in his memory

were they ordered, real, hugely present.
It was a mercy, then, that his circuitry
should be clotted as with dust, and his eyes
blind to the spectacle of a body—his own—

sprawling across the prim gravel verge,
jutting over the carefully clipped lawn,
while we trampled the flowers to reach him
and the rockery cast its indifferent shadows.

Thalia

I loved the canted catwalk
in my grandfather's little movie hall,
which the local chapter
of the New Africa Movement
rented for meetings—vibrant,
sub rosa, doubtless illegal—

while my brother and sister and I
spied through the fascinating
helical bars of the tilted railing.

My brother was an Army sergeant,
my sister a WAC nurse,
and I the Vietnamese orphan
that they battled over:
either the nurse would save me
or the sergeant throw me alive
on a Viet Cong funeral pyre.

(This was before My Lai.)

Below us they debated whether
a downtown riot was the way to go
or a conflagration in the suburbs.

How passionately the tall man
in the blue dashiki inveighed
against "the jackbooted sons
of Japheth," an adversary
I was relieved to learn
included no one in my family.

We watched without fear,
until someone said, "Hey, you!"—
and we fled down the catwalk,
down the hawing stairs,

and into Grandma's kitchen.

On the linoleum counter,
among ordinary dishes
still steaming from the range—
bitter melon, soy-sauce chicken,
salted fish, lotus-root soup—

lay an exotic, congealed pile
of ham hocks and greens
on a chipped Grand Canyon plate,

an offering left that afternoon—
with the rent in cash—
by the solicitous wife
of Grandpa's most reliable tenant.

Tempo

One definition of marriage: *what remains after two people*
spend a lifetime slaying each other. While I was admiring
the brindled koi in Grandpa's lotus pond, he and Grandma
were screaming in the living room, in the master bedroom,
in bedrooms two and three and four where children
five through eight slept; lettuce leaves were flying, I remember,
in red-fingered pizzicato against the kitchen window,
and then the filling for the lettuce leaves, pink strains of chicken,
mutilated chords of shiitake and bamboo shoot,
which I later saw them wiping away, side by side.
Another definition of marriage: *a state in which one discovers*
what is most subservient in oneself and compels it fervently
at the Other. One day my father and I happened upon
my mother weeping in her sewing room, and both of us
consoled her until I sensed, in her high-pitched iterations
(droning trills, lunging fortissimos), that she demanded
solace I couldn't give, so I withdrew to the living room,
where I put on some Brahms. In the hush that flowed
between the orchestra and the flights of the piano,
I heard my father say she should skip her exploratory
surgery, never mind he'd become a widower, he'd learn
to take care of the children and the house while putting in
twelve hours a day at his store plus the commute;
and as he wept, I heard my mother reply, *No, no,*
you'd make an awful widower, you'd set my kitchen
on fire, I'll go to the hospital, I won't die on the table
after all, my poor house'd fall apart . . . And so it went,
the fearful music of my beloved adults, whose instructions
I spent much of my life trying to forget, only to find them
scored on my heart: *presto, appassionato, con molto*
espressione, più agitato.

Grandfather Writes His Will

Trout bones on a gray-blue plate, fine
as larch needles. Shadow on a rib cage, rib bones
holding it back like a hand. What pierces
the X-ray reaches out to you like a hand, raven-clawed,
digging in, digging in.

Dinner over, a walk in the twilit park
across the street. The air tom-tomming with currents
of cool and warm—not Indian summer, not autumn.
A woman in a yellow sari, small-boned, graceful,
walks down a leaf-strewn path. You want to touch
each lozenge in the fabric before it blurs
in memory, becomes a shadow on a rib cage.
Everything these days is a shadow on a rib cage.

And what of the monkey bars? What of the scoop
of hazelnut ice cream? One heaped high like a sarcophagus,
clutching the sky to flesh-eating stone;
the other tasting of earth you will "return to."
Did you ever leave it? Carpet beneath your feet,
eight little snapshots—your grown children—
dangling from the gilded branches
of a little family tree.

The lights are on in your house, and no one hears
the scratch, scratch, scratch of your pen.

Black Screen

A leaf, orbicular, enflamed with autumn,
fell to my windshield, like the afterimage that scarred
the air before my eyes: I flicked a switch,

and it was gone. Across the city I kept the radio off,
dreading the tidal plunge and scourge of witness:
It is human nature to stand in the middle of a thing,

but you cannot stand in the middle of this.
At the azalea cul-de-sac by my childhood home,
I parked my car and stepped through riffling gravel

to the old immutable lawn. The den lights
cast a familiar radiance that spilled
across the open border to where golden footlights

shone a path through the neighbor's yard—
the light of the past, of *pax vobiscum.*
Now distant skyscrapers worried the frame

of windows on my brother's van, and the old mower
lay foreshortened on its side, its undercarriage
a black rectangle with circular teeth,

the maw of the void. Those late seasons spent
reading in the yard, longing for nothing more
than "the sexy airs of summer": nothing itself

was not the same. From the patio I watched
my family watch the screen within the screen
of the sliding-glass doors. Turned away

(in a moment canting sideways to greet me
against the angle of the television set),
they gazed through an electronic suspension

of fire and ashes, my brother on the edge
of the ottoman, my sister cradling a glass of wine,
my gangly nephew sprawled on the carpet.

Behind my mother's wheelchair, my father clutched
the handholds, both of them shaking their heads
as the planes hit the towers again and again,

and when, for a moment, the screen went dark
I glimpsed the same tearful reflection that I saw
in the idle heart monitor the night the doctor

unhooked my grandfather and pronounced him dead.

Salt

The sun is a Tudor arch sustaining the sky.
In a moment it will fall. Blackbirds
with crimson suns on their wings
squawk in protest, and my sister,
in lovely, billowy clothes from Anticipation,
picks a sky-blue cornflower that she'll press
between pages of the O.E.D.

In the lightless vault of words
the petal tips will caress
an adjective from the Old French.

Now, as she strays through the field,
she asks me if she's beginning to look like
Ophelia—she doesn't know why,
she just imagines Ophelia long-haired
and pregnant—and I say, "No, no,
you're a terrible singer and much too sane,"

and she pulls her ample sleeves
together in a solemn, mandarin way
and bows to the birds startling
the sky and bows to the dying sun
and bows to me, her younger brother,
who wants nothing more of the world
than to salt the stream before her
that she may float and float
and never drown.

Red Rattlesnake

The day I looked at nursing homes I nearly stepped
on it. Supple, deliquescent, as if dipped

in a viscous film of paraffin, rust-red,
it coiled on a rust-red sandstone bed,

sloughing itself, I thought, or posed to strike—
I couldn't tell, halted mid-hike

in its glass-bead stare. Nothing
existed but the solipsism of my fear, or everything

I knew contracted to the vision: diamond-faïence
pattern ending in a suspended rattle, soundless,

not red but milky-blue, undipped like Achilles' heel,
in scaly dishabille . . .

When I tell my mother, she barely hears me. "A story,"
her face says. "I'm beyond stories."

So I stop and give her the rundown:
Verde Vista a cheerless green, Saguaro Downs

OK if unclean, Desert Home for the Infirm and Aged—
isn't the name itself tactless? She looks enraged,

or maybe it's swelling from the steroids.
I raise a spoonful of cherry applesauce, avoid

her angry gape. She chews in a trance,
Mummy Mountain reclining in the distance.

Enraged at what was done to her—but by whom?
Time or fate or the whim

of a god who reduced her body
to this soundless aria, this mortal threnody,

under the inferno's garish proscenium.
Give me the faith to sing a scornless *Te Deum*,

to chant *Holy, holy, holy,* to the maker of the flesh, now tensed
in rictus, that once possessed a godly immanence,

turning the scales on any childhood chagrin
with a joy, anodyne, incarnate, my second skin.

The Similes

After we found the kindly young woman who would stay
in my sister's old bedroom and take care of you
"like family," after we gave her your old TV set
and splurged on a flat-screened monitor and a phone
with voice recognition that would dial for you
like the fingers you could no longer use, after we installed
the electric lift with its sleek black ladle and its straps
and pulleys dangling from a steel track on the ceiling—
"like a Disney ride," my brother said;
"like a torture chamber," you murmured—
we saw that you hated everything we had done,
hated the adjustable bed like the one
in the nursing home you'd keened to get out of,
hated the lift over the bed, like a strappado
for a recalcitrant witch, hated the beautiful screen
with its preternatural clarity, like a mockery
of the visionary opacities that had arrived
with old age, hated most of all
the young woman with her cherubic dimples,
which you wanted to press in "like sponge cake,"
and her harmless love of spinach: "like Popeye?"
you inquired.

At the corner café the three children held a summit,
"like Yalta," my sister said, dryly. How angry we were,
our love swatted away like Zuleika Dobson's suitors
or maybe Yukiko's in *The Makioka Sisters*.
Afterward we brought you a chocolate cake,
slipping a Re-Admit Form for the nursing home
under the knot of the pastry box, like a reminder card
from the dentist. "Like an extortion letter,"
you corrected, but grew kinder to the gentle nurse,

who stayed beyond the trial period, to our relief.
"Like the child I never had," you said at Christmas
as she fed you a morsel of lamb.

Doorknob

An old brass doorknob, scuffed from keys, from turning,
the half-dozen times she jostled it each time we left
the house, and the final twist my father made

running back from the car at her command: I see her
in the pathos of scuff marks, the sanctuary of home
inseparable from the anxiety of its custody.

I refused to perform the ritual when asked,
teased my father for his shrugging assent,
for looking back at her and jiggling the knob again,

the uxorious gaze it would take me decades
to admire and, at last, to mourn. Now my brother
undrills the screws and pops out the knobs

and latch cylinder and jamb, all so flimsy—
"and there's no deadbolt," he says. "A burglar
could've shouldered it open." With a drill bit

he gouges a quadrilateral in the soft wood
on the jamb, following pilot holes
from a paper template pressed against the bevel.

Now he assembles the deadbolt's double cylinder,
an internal clinking of aureate rounds and screws
where the key will go each day, as if storing up

the daily music my father will make when he leaves
the house to push my mother's wheelchair
along sidewalks shaded with looming ficus and ash.

On good days her failing eyes will gaze through leaves
at a sunset flecked scarlet like a blood orange,
and peel away the sky to find a blued blackness mottled

with stars, and he'll accept her tranquility as the will
to live, not the relinquishment that jars us now
each time she crosses the threshold and says nothing.

Counterprayer

Let me not mourn you before you die—this is something I can write,
not utter. If I spoke, the labyrinth in your ear
would straighten out the words I said. ("Blessed is the son
who prematurely mourns," you'd laugh
as I wept.) But if I wrote, the cloud in your eyes would see
soft-hued runes on a shivered codex, bleared ideograms, the radical
for "man" leaning against the character for "two," comforting
as a mother. Let me not think of you in the past tense either:
how you *waited* as Father and I stared at the baggage carousel,
how your chair *slid* backwards along an endlessly receding airport
    ramp,
how you *uttered* a wan and cheerful "Wheeeeeee!"
before toppling over. No, I won't mourn your good humor
or the wheel spinning in the air as the crowd converged to help
my crippled mother. I won't mourn the word "crippled"
or the word "my." I'll wait until after your ears
no longer buzz, until after my own hand is crippled,
and I'll summon an absence and place it round each word
I can no longer write, and it will be your absence
that I will utter, forever and never,
without amen.

Word

The high sweep of waves, like the bulging arc
of a grand piano, and the silence of deer in a field of
lupine and trefoil, and the underthrum
of the engine turning a switchback back
to the city—"afternoon fog," the announcer warns,
each new sea vista reverting to redwoods, back
and forth, back and forth, as if we were tracing
the sinuous legato of the Schumann trio
on the car radio.

Today the patches of sunlit mist that flow in
through the foothills and obscure the filigree
on a row of Queen Annes are occlusions
from my mother's CT-scan: that steel-blue blur
on blur of cortex and wine-dark hemorrhage.
A year after her stroke they've flown out
for their anniversary, the otherworldly monotone
of her "aprosodia" leaving her wary of voicing
the love of new scenery with anything more
than a tactful coo and purl,

until we emerge from the last tunnel to where
the bridge's gargantuan red suspensions
loom between a lowering mist and the bleared
upswell of blond hills, showing a mere tendril
of red cables and one tower's massive tuning fork,
uncanny, oddly collate, but enough for her
to stutter, "Beauti-, beauti-, beauti-,"

a word my father completes with a whisper:
"-ful, -ful, -ful."

My Mother's Hands

Now that she's ashamed of their ancient burls and gibbous knobs—
"Don't be ashamed!" I cry—
I find myself staring at the raw matter of their decay,
nails crumbling to the opalescent grit
of their lunulae, liver spots speckling the dorsal vein
with its throbbing blue limbs, as if the leopard,
symbol of lust in Dante, lay panting, enfeebled,
in the dark wood.

I can't bear that these hands won't always be here,
though I barely noticed them when they were still dexterous,
commanding me to come here, do this chore, listen to this
sweet story, come here, sweetheart, come here . . .

Now a scythelike rod planted within the same index finger
gives it an incongruous come-hither look that forces
passersby to point to themselves, thinking
she's beckoning to them, an optical illusion, of course,
like the Beauty and the Crone.

"This hand is not the crux and matter of you," I want to say,
but know she'd laugh and ask, "Is it what's the matter
with you?" or—worse—look away in pain, saying,
"It doesn't matter, it doesn't matter."

And so I hold on tight as she sits in her wheelchair, as if
to guide her somewhere, anywhere, until I kiss her goodbye,
and her hands fall from my own to a spot on her desk
by the gift my father gave her when they were young:
a glass paperweight, clear, abstract, voluptuous,
with five sparkling air bubbles clutching
a bouquet of clouds.

OOO

My Demeter

Afternoons I fall asleep without meaning to.
The sun draws aside the white curtain, and the sea,
the sea is "veined with liquid fire," like Milton's hell.
Figures—gods or lost friends or the dead—
shuttle between the foot of my bed and the hole
in a fulgurous cloud, pale-yellow, like brimstone.
A woman says, "How can I bear to live
if I can no longer see my mother?"
A man says, "Then go back. Think of yourself
as a season. Think you will live
to die to live."

Now something shivers into the room,
a specter or a snowdrift or a poem inhabiting
the same quadrant of the mind as the love
a boy feels for a mother suddenly old,
one last season caressing the snowy hair,
winter's rime crinkling outward
from the underworld in her eyes.

II

The Eye

After-echo of sirens, a sliding-glass door, curtains
parting, the dark-green room with the white bed,
the tiny spot of blood on the useless tube
in her throat. Eyes closed; we never closed them
for her. "Sleep is sleep," she'd scoff, which meant
death was not a dozing lamb. And yet I opened
one lid to expose a dead eye, empty and glassen
as the sweet beast's gaze. I wanted one last look in,
but it didn't stay open. Something, not my touch,
closed it for her again, something, mere inertia,
reflex of the orbicular oculi, something that defied
the solace of metaphor, the succor of half-truths
she taught us to resist, like the words I uttered
to console my father: "She wants to stay asleep."

The Parrot

The week after my mother died, my sight turned
arid, monochrome. The distressed-bronze casket
she chose, the peach and vermilion pied roses
on her wreaths, the floral fripperies of her dress—
all drained out of me, like my tears. The cortège
glided through dappled puddles, but I saw nothing,
rehearsing her eulogy like a desperate parrot
praised by its masters for a childlike intelligence.
I spoke as if each sentence austerely repeated
the austere repetitions of some inhuman engine
of meaning, and the faces of my loved ones
floated in crepuscular gauze, as if I were hooded
by godlike captors who replaced the rain forest
with a sterile white room and a large wire cage.

The Colors

Like her, I have a taste for the dark—the green
not of sun-soaked silver linden leaves,
but the same in leaf shadow, or if in sunlight,
the sea-dark red sfumato that glows through
a wicker Chianti on a sidewalk café table,
the same color she wore that day on the Sound,
its blue-mussel waves like the steaming ones
in our serving pail, a row of dark nacred morsels
she lovingly left on my plate. When she died,
I wept over the things she left me one by one
during her last year: the tarnished silver,
the pocket watch's sliver of deep-green jade,
the maroon wallet that stored our snapshots
in a snap pouch, unfaded, safe, in the dark.

The Images

Not the light as interpreted by electron or xenon,
not the step-by-step arrangement of twig and morsel
on a rectangular Japanese dish with legs,
not the pixel-augmented pulchritude,
not the terminal glib, the white rictus extruding
the petrified word, not the specious salute to a helicopter,
the hollered question from behind a velvet rope,
not the broken minaret aside the shiny red Jaguar—
nothing wounds me more than a last memory
of my mother squinting into the sunlight
as we waited in the car, how I held my hand up
to shade her eyes, as she shielded me once
from the daze and dazzle of the world
by turning off the TV set.

The Names

Neither a phantom's chill, sub-woofer keen
nor the high *cri de cœur* of a spectral belle dame,
my name, broken into tiny shards and soughs,
rattled me more than any ghost in chains.
A living apparition (though what haunted me
was a vision of grief), she'd speed-dial me,
her good hand lifting the phone as she called out
the word that was her gift to me. I waited gladly,
even as I feared the unmediated fragmentation
of tone—self-generated static, syntax perched
on a broken dendrite—which I expected still
to slip into the voice I knew, clear, precipitate,
like an emergency operator who breaks in
to say your name and that of one you love.

The Dove

Among the pigeons outside the hospital was one
I would give the pure white name, beyond motley
or the darting saurian gawp that leaves my sister,
with her lifelong fear of birds, in a fret. I didn't say
how the beautiful dove reminded me of our mother
lying under a last white bedsheet, her face soft
under our last kisses, as I imagined the plush down
of the dove. Sunlight on my father's cheek,
the back of my brother's neck, brought out
the living glow she still possessed, hidden now
in the mortician's bag as his van pulled away.
Not much longer, I morbidly thought, before cold
and marmoreal sheen undid the memory of flight
from the pulseless veins. The dove flew away.

The Catfish

Afterward I held my sister but not him.
It was enough that we possessed the same voice;
I didn't want to be lost in him, like a figure
in facing mirrors. I only wept, later, recalling
our mother, and then only by phone. I needed
the fiber-optic refuge, imagining him as myself
listening to his double sobbing into a grid
of bundled light, like a lachrymose Mondrian.
Later I apologized, and he said, "Don't worry
about it," as he did the time we were children
and I startled to see the dying fish he fetched
in a bucket of river water clouded with blood:
the whiskered head rose once to the surface,
stoic, benumbed, then sank slowly under.

The Deer

I know you had to leave without saying when
or goodbye. Beyond my tears the corridor
holds my sister's face, my father's hands,
like wobbling planets in a little telescope.
I want to speak to you, but the questions
are gestures torn from flesh and impulse,
like the deer we saw at a trickling flume
along the trail: the words startle and leap
into the mists of the forest. If I could,
I'd tell you how winter subsided in a warm,
claustral room full of memories we never
spoke of again, so brief they were, and final,
how I hushed to follow your awestruck gaze
as he bounded through the wild strawberries.

III

Empty Room

A faint pink-gray lamp, tincture of rose and iodine,
in the apartment across the street: serious light,
the kind where "scenes" take place. I wonder
what fixtures store sells it, what melancholy
factory assembles it. It may be backwash
from wallpaper chosen in the most delicate
of compromises: sailing vessels
of dark-purplish hue arrayed in equal measure
with sprays of white flowers, hemlock perhaps,
pinked under lampshade fringes. Conflict
is easy to imagine, even in distant emptiness.
And what are the yellow lumps on the coffee table?
Quinces, fruit of the rose, a single bite
taken from each. The white splotch? A doily,
ovate from this angle, bleeding grayly on the mantelshelf,
like a wound. And the oblong cabinet?
A Renaissance sideboard, a credence, with faces carved
in each panel: Joy and Grief and Desire
and, rigged to pour gin, the grave smile
of Alienation. What credence to place in what I see?
None, perhaps. It's useless, a friend once told me,
to think about other people's inner lives.
But what if there are no people
in the inner life? Only their traces, unclearly seen,
full of shadow and mystery—what then?
And how to stop from thinking, from puzzling,
late at night, the stars turning above the clouds
above my head?

A hand—the face and body out of view—
reaches for the lamp and flicks the light switch off.

The Toaster

The elements, square and coppery, spill out,
like memento mori for toast. I'd await
my slices, reading the dense page of a classic,
till I heard the pop and savored a golden melt
so painless it helped me digest the morsel
I learned. In my youth I aimed to be
my own Axial Age: vacuous as Buddha,
disputatious as Socrates, deferential
to my ghosts as Confucius. And all along
a dropped toaster could have told me how
time's white dial falls away, how metal baffles
twist into a question mark, how a spring
from an ejection knob uncoils to infinity,
how a crumb tray weeps its earthly fragments.

White Canopy

(From a Line by Lope de Vega)

You, you, writing epitaphs for the living,
with a little Ion-brand pen that opens like a casket,
your body a pool of blue-black ink in a clear vitrine,
what is posterity but a tiny shard of your mirror?
The words are Spanish cypresses planted as inchlings
to impale the unburied through the heart, and you alone
recline under a sheer white baldachin, listening
to a flamenco guitar carved from cypress wood.
Forget the black pillow on your dead mother's wheelchair
or the wire-rimmed glasses your late Grandpa Tom wore:
you lie there, myopically, taking notes on the living—
the embrittled bones of your aunt, your father's
failing memory—as if your words could ever be
the solace of calcium or ginkgo biloba.

Hermit Crab

He sniffs the briny vanilla aroma on the dropcloth
spattered with glaucous-sapphire paint drying now
on the walls and stanchions, and—landlocked—visits
a city by the sea, its law school, its bayside towers,
which he hasn't seen since the day two decades ago
he chose this life of revision and attentive regret.
Now he paints these sea-touched walls as homage
to the world beyond the horny pagurian self
on which he projects tears from the world beyond,
like a homely *lacrimæ rerum*. "But there are no tears,"
he tells himself, rinsing the contorted brushes
in a white bucket that soon fills with the colors
of the ocean as a writer sees them, stilled, proximate,
awaiting the words that would make them weep.

The Solitary

The room held, as if condensed, honey-olive shadows
from the canopy that stretched over bamboo
scaffolding across the window. Titles of books,
the rose pattern on an amulet, all the objects
not directly under the corner lamp were khaki-tinted,
hard to see. Just visible beyond a folding screen,
the bed had a dark, military air, as if the beige-brown
comforter were a hard, medieval pavis. The balcony,
with a southern exposure, was brighter, but blocked
by plants and stacks of books, so that it too
had the look of something fortified, a section
of a parapet, perhaps, or the lower half of a bartizan,
with a long, red, snakelike banner flying somewhere
on the roof. The Smith Corona, black under the lamp,
bore a jagged crack that extended from the "Shift" key
to a spot below the letter "V," legacy of an incident
whose details remain murky, except that it was
"defenestrated" one morning. (The word said
with a blithe, sideways glance, as if to challenge
the listener.) Then, in the middle of the room,
the great Bible on its wooden analogion,
built to specifications he carried with him from
country to country. So far: Russia, Arabia,
Senegal, China. I had barely enough time
on this, my only visit, to see where the bookmark,
a sandalwood dagger, flagged the day's meditation,
when he returned with a lacquer tray
and green tea in tiny porcelain cups decorated
with blue insects—"gadflies," he called them.
Later, I looked it up: "Ye shall be free indeed,"
the verses said, a flicker of light from the fortress.

The Relinquishing

One by one she relinquished her friends, then moved away,
taking her series of lithographs. For hours we'd pose
before zinc sheets accreting a thousand swift gestures,
our features winnowed, thinned, abstracted, the air feathery

behind our torsos, like Giacomettis with wings. She called them—
and us, by extension—her "dark angels," but it was no surprise
that she was the one to fly away. East, then farther east:
one day a postcard from Suzdal, Russia, with a vestigial hello.

Sometimes I think of her arriving among us, ringletted, wispy,
reading Plato, practicing German. Her measured *voice* ("*Stimme,*"
she'd say) evoked an *atmosphere* ("*Stimmung,* same root"),
serious, a bit pedantic, balanced by the kindly half-smile

that drew you back to her as she extended a pea pod
or a blue-green seaweed cracker. We'd sit on a beach
while the others unpacked the volleyball net, and she'd sigh
as it rose over the sand, and speak of Socrates' vision

of great ropes of light, purer and more lucent than rainbows,
from whose extremities the spindle of Necessity turned. Later,
she spent more and more time in her loft, alone, aloof;
"it's *necessary,*" her explanation. True, all of us adored art,

lived for its sparks of vision, promised to forgo a dozen
easy futures to traverse its doubtful terrain, but her ambition
was something silent and obdurate, a rain hood that flew past me
one rainless day, a shadow pacing behind some curtains,

as if she were rehearsing the fateful and needless solitude
for which one last postcard imparted the glossy proof:
a room in a monastery, with three radiant looms
and a dark cowl hanging on a wall, like a retracted wing.

Fiber Optics

Again a call from an old friend I thought I'd lost,
the name sheepishly uttered, the pause, the rush
of joy liquefying the wires:

the long draft imbibed, savored,
of common names, Albert's mother's remarriage, Sandra's
promotion, Jeremiah—when did Jeremiah change his name to
Steve? And the flow of explanations
into which we dip—of home, of work, of love,
how it's a mere mockup of a river, a silvery ether
made of tinfoil shaken by Props from the wings of the stage,
not a real river, not real life,

but that doesn't explain why
we never talked till now. Why now? Why not next year?
Certainly it's as if nothing had changed; we swim smoothly
through years and jobs and days, drifting back
to the familiar waters of our estrangement
only when you go off to fetch your address book.

How hard the ear works to make out the background noise,
the clink of the coffee mug, the chatter of Sunday papers,
how hard it presses against the ear-warmed disk
to discern—what? The click of a hanger emptying
its mundane load? The VCR switching on by itself?
How weary the sounds that stumble across the wire—
the old address penciled out, the new address
penciled in—and everything clear,
static-free, instantaneous, flowing true,
by long-distance fiber optics.

The Sparrow

Holding him—briefly—in my palm,
a pyramid of birdseed in the center,
I'm tickled by a slick covert of wing
and grayish nape that are the wind
and sky in motion, soft on my lifeline
crinkling under his skittish beak.
He is the line that divides seeing
from unseeing, the instant flapped
and flung weightless to its own loss,
all dart and glint and breasted puff
graying the eye with intricate choice
devised in braincase and neural stem
small as sprouted edamame.
For an instant he flings the infinite
peripheries where life is lived
into the conscious center where life
is interpreted, just as a thinking
cloud might center the withered sage
contemplating nothingness under
a last cloudy extrusion among
the sacred peaks, just as we still
ourselves from the time-lapse
flickering of the beloved each time
it lights on us to escape downtown,
replace troth, fond and frazzled,
with street scenes: the peripheral
glamour of a shop window, the way
the corner sushi bar reprises
some ancient praise of darkness,
the face of a beautiful stranger
under a recessed light's glow

intervening, for an instant,
between the tiny, fleeting self
and the end of possibility.

Pattern

The rug folded back with a sweep of your hand, revealing
parquetry inlaid with a pattern of sharp, elongated teeth.
Your mother had loved it. *My teeth fell out,* she'd say,
and became part of the house! After she died,

> you never really settled in. Even the kitschy things—
> the little sampan and cormorant, the Modigliani pastiche—
> were hard to dump. I watched you lug them to the cellar
> one by one, solemnly, without relief. For a year

you humored the antimacassars, fingered them gingerly, the lace
smarmy with her memory. Like a therapist, I'd ask you to draw up
a list of debits and credits: what was gained, what lost,
in baring the arms of the sofa. The look on your face

> was pained, but one day you declared, "It's not enough
> to hide them anymore"—and I knew you'd decided to give up
> the house and all its doleful bric-a-brac. That evening,
> during dinner, you vanished into her favorite room,

your place suddenly vacant, a plate of angel-hair pasta left
steaming on the table. The thought of angels, even angel hair,
had turned the talk to Rilke, and your face bore the poet's
lugubrious intensity. You could have been perched on a cliff

> of Ronda in a storm, turning the ineffable into words,
> as you peered over the upturned corner of your rug.
> It didn't matter that the rug had its own associations—
> your bleak, glorious year in Harbin, your special trip

to some dusty factory in Inner Mongolia, your own flower-tangled
design scrawled on scratch paper in the manager's yurt; you saw
only what was covered, what was muted, your mother's teeth
shrouded by the cool, handwoven fibers, the losses,

> only the losses. And as I leaned over to touch your
> shoulder, our voices rose at the same time—mine
> to comfort you and bring you back to me, yours to seek
> for comfort—canceling each other out in midair

like an interference pattern, love's dazzled, dazzling imbrications.

At the Palace of Fine Arts

"I'll die," Nathalie pleaded, "if I don't see him,"
but this was the fourth iteration of the futile game,
and I'd be damned if I'd waste gas money—a quarter?
a nickel?—to backtrack to that indifferent brute's
third-floor window above Sutter Street,
where he nudely lifted weights in full view
of ex-lovers and other connoisseurs of muscle.
We were penny-pinching bohemians, she *une jeune fille*
un peu folle, with a see-through telephone,
a taste for scarlet—scarlet shoes, book bags,
cat collar—and one lost-wax earring that sheared
right through the lobe. I gave my last savings
to the plastic surgeon to repair it, payment
for the right, I thought, to refuse the foolish exigencies
of her aloneness. Instead, I drove straight
to the fake museum with its fake columns
(concrete, Corinthian) and its manmade pond,
so charming at dusk. "Forget him," I repeated softly
as she trembled and wept. Just visible
in the failing light, the temporary "sculpture,"
a hidden machine that lowered the violet surface
of the water with a man-sized hexahedron
of air. "The same shape as a coffin or a bed,"
I suggested. *"La même chose,"* she replied,
with a melancholy so vehement that I began
to laugh, and she, hearing herself, joined in,
until we had scared something dark and winged
across the water and into the echoing night.

Synapse

*Darknesse and light divide the course of time, and oblivion shares with
memory, a great part even of our living beings; we slightly remember
our felicities, and the smartest stroaks of affliction leave but short smart
upon us.*

 —Thomas Browne, *Hydriotaphia, or Urne-Buriall*

"It's a construct," she said. Like *everything*? No, like lecture notes.
You pick a subject ("Death from the Renaissance
to the Restoration," "The Nervous Breakdown
in Popular Culture"), survey a hundred books, a thousand.
Certain qualities possess you: Veracity, Tenderness,
Morbidity, Zeal. You shape your notes,
elide them, distend them, rework them year by year
until one day the pages shiver and blur, and you're left
with a bruise-colored *idée fixe* from a past
composed of texts: your boyish fervor for *Zen and the Art
of Motorcycle Maintenance*, your grave enchantment
with *Urne-Buriall*.

"'If only I hadn't read the list of symptoms . . .'—is that it?"
He gazed at the Laughing Buddha, akimbo to globular belly,
which blocked the fireplace, and asked, "Are we talking about
'a condition ultimately requiring faith'? If so, I'm undone."
"Faith and more" was the answer that was not an answer.
He could hear the next patient turning the pages
of the coffee-table books in the alcove outside—he could hear the *pages*,
Impressionists from Chicago, soothing Renoirs, Hokusais,
and in the grim collection at the bottom of the stack,
a self-portrait of Dürer pointing to his own spleen.

Another day the Buddha was set aside, and there was a fire,
and rain outside, and thunder, and no electricity. "Eerie,"

he said, "your voice coming from the shadows." (Also, palliative—
he'd call her answering machine just to hear her murmur,
If it's an emergency, call my pager number . . .) "Can you see my face?"
she asked. "I see yours. It's sort of dappled and moving;
you look wonderfully *externalized.*"
He muttered, "Darknesse and light divide the course of my face . . ."
"I meant it as praise," she explained. "People who never display
the contents of their minds are incapable of changing them."
And then, bemused: "Something you'll want to take with you
on the 'outside,' don't you think?"

He took the kitchen knife and sliced half a dose for starters,
but the white inner powder was friable, like cocaine.
He brought his nose up close to smell; no smell.
What if it lingered on the tongue, an acrid burn?
Would the association undo the anodyne effect he expected—
no, had *faith in?* Particles clung to the whorls of his finger,
slipped in the clear insipid, hinting of something sweet
but not always so: an extract of infancy diluted
to a part per million. All afternoon he checked the view
across the rooftops, straining to see a change
though he knew it would take weeks, the revolving vent
still a mad scolex suckling on the sky, the transmission tower—
red-eyed, robotic—astride the same hill punctured
by houses on stilts: pretty as a Thai fishing village, he decided,
though others whispered, "Cancer cluster." Above the city
the sun was a burning oval on the back of a deflected retina,
and a high-altitude plane made a sleek line through it,
like the sign for *null.* As the contrail vanished,
it turned into the prescription she wrote—
a classic doctor's hand, fleet, southpaw, illegible—
on the little pad she kept by her armchair.

Asperger

He stares at the chromatic riffle of banners
on a museum, the esprit of aqua, the dolor
of violet, spectral translucencies
high above, where the wind, embodied,
dances a tireless divertimento.
Closer by, the ginkgo's bark is a city
of wood-grained byways, tenements
whose grid of shuttered windows conceals
some tiny, distant ronde of lovers:
and a man and a woman, and a woman and
a woman, and a woman and a man, and . . .

He is staring, staring: the unreal self
in the zinc counter's bleared reflection,
the dusky whorl on cappuccino foam
that discloses another expired name for God,
lost with a dip of the spoon.

What is a person next to a thing? If he could,
he would return your gaze and hold it forever,
fixing on an iris, gilled and clandestine
under the transparent dome of the cornea,
like a mushroom's upturned pileus
sealed in some radiant miniature
of the earth's atmosphere.

No, the blue day speaks only of things.
The pigeon's wing, upside-down, rights itself
inside his brain. The cloud's face confides,
I know you love me. When he leans over
his sketch pad to draw the arrangement
on the café table, he is no longer a person

but the thing itself, a hollowed-out culm,
green and plumb and punctiliously jointed:

bamboo bamboo bamboo bamboo bamboo

Red Sandstone Cliffs at Dusk

The sound of human suffering in the distance—
a contralto, wailing lavishly—comes from a bearing
off the mountain that places it in the stand
of solitary shacks by the airport—a hermit's
lurid caterwaul—until you locate it among
the echoing rocks so close by you can make out
the stippled hackles she raises, in righteous fury,
to lover or foe unseen around a bend
in the trail, a scene, perhaps a tragedy,
so enthralling she doesn't notice the outsider
listening for signs of what she means, as if
a feral cat might divulge something I've sought
to isolate, something fearful and telling,
which may tell of nothing but isolation.

Singularities

In Portola Valley, south of San Francisco,
I saw a bobcat once. He was not very large,
perhaps the size of my neighbor's small collie,
and he gazed at me benignly, the tan markings
and tawny tufts blending skillfully
into the dry California hillside.
A gnarly ancient madroño, with a bough
whose twisted surface seemed to carry souls
in limbo, cast a blue shadow
over both of us, and it was unnerving,
unlike the bobcat himself, that we should stand
in the shade of the same tree.
I had time to notice that he was perched
on a clump of reddening poison oak
and to wonder if he were somehow immune,
as I in my long running sweats hoped
myself to be, and I noticed, minuscule
against his magnified presence, the purple blur
of a royal larkspur, inexplicably abloom
in the heat, gaping like a wound
in search of the paw's thorn.
I don't know how long I stared into
his brown, clever eyes, how long I waited
for the awful to happen, even as I knew
it would not happen. That's when,
for no reason, he startled, drew a clear zigzag
on the air, and bounded sleekly, silently,
up his feline path. I turned back
to my human trail, edging familiar curves
amidst miner's lettuce and cool allium,
reaching at last the bluff where I could see,
in the middle of a brilliant green ridge,

a fir tree towering above the other firs,
and closer by, at my feet, a spider's web
like an upside-down umbrella, bright
and iridescent, with a small brown spider
at the center, also upside down,
feeding in silence on iridescent prey.

The Madness of Ajax

The open field at whose end he glowered, panting;
blue thistle crumpling under white paws spraying dust;
rope carving into blue-black poll, seared pink-red;
fog and cliffs, indifferent, as in a scroll by Kuo Hsi—
I whispered into the cell phone to Animal Control,
sealing the fate of one who knew the anger and insult
of a god who had left him tormented, lashing out
at those he would love, like an artist whose clutch
of conventions he twists and tortures, in each vision,
to a lasting figure, his only revenge the masters
he slays with original beauty. Beyond the field
the trail led down to a stream where we drank wine
and recited our favorite sonnets. Art is the murder
you lovingly repeat until you craft its final harm.

The Candle

It's raining. A pluvial wheeze, a floating cloud
like a pneumonectomy, then a greenish sun in a Whirlpool-brand
agitator. So muggy I can't help thinking, "I'm going to die,"
then clutching my sides with the agita
of my amateur theatrics. Funny too the circular thought
that I'm a single gasping pore composed of countless millions
    combined

into one wheezing passage—from the Greek *poros,* passage, which in
    combin-
ation with the privative α- yields the cloud
of nubilous feeling or thwarted thought
called *aporia.* Doubt is the frat-house brand
I saw on the reality-show contestant's muscularly agita-
ted shoulder as he panicked during the sudden-death

playoff: failing to unlock a lock underwater while an adversary cried,
    "Def!"
I see him twenty or thirty years from now in the foolish bind
of being forced each time he checked the mirror to recall his
    youthful agita-
tion to achieve unreflective union with a cloud
of likenesses.—Or not: as he surfaces, gasping, the Greek letters of
    the brand
glistening hotly, he thinks

(in voice-over), "I'm still a winner. I've always thought
myself a winner. I always will." Better to throw a single die
into an abyss or huddle over a smoldering brand
in some northern desert—tundra, badlands, rusting combines—
like my friend Jarrett's boyfriend's friend Heinz, who hitchhiked to
    St. Cloud
or Compulsion Bay, bringing only the *Bhagavad-Gita*

and his bare Teutonic chin. A failure, of course. The *Gita*
instructed, "Focusing his mind on the self, he should think
nothing." But *nothing* never happened. Lonely, bearded, still occlud-
ed, he returned to New York, *die Stadt des Todes,* the City of Death,
where he tagged neologistic combin-
ing forms in red gel-ink rollerball, Gelly Roll brand—

i.e., became a proofreader. Happiness was not a volcano spewing
    bright-red *Brand-*
fluß over the soul. It was here, there, now and again, nowhere, agita
and quietude in fiery combin-
ation, like the "red-phosphorescent jellyfish" Elizabeth Bishop thought
she saw from her high window on the beach in Rio, which died
as she stepped into the sand to reach it, becoming a cloud

of someone's religious feeling bound to *macumba,* or a thought-
ful indicator—when extinguished—of the tide's agitated swell, or a
    vision of death,
luminous, then dark, the only brand for the doubtful, who live and
    die in a cloud.

Ballad of Infinite Forgetfulness

(After Hugo von Hofmannsthal)

And strangers will arrive as they'll depart, shaking your hand,
And friends will say, "Sorry," and walk right through you,
And thought will slip through a sieve, honeyed with sadness.

And lovers will spin in the windows of a cinquefoil,
And minutes will stream like corpuscles through the streets
Until they're caught in a frontage road labeled, "No Outlet."

And dogs will listen for a master who'll never return,
For a garage door to rise at the touch of a remote control,
For the latch to unlock and the presence of a god to enter in.

And a god will throw down a fog that clarifies, not obscures,
And leaves will grow clear and have no need to fall,
And a root-sphere will pulse in the clear ground, like a mind.

And your father will grow senile and fretful, and your mother
Will lose the strength to lift the side of her hand,
And the gravedigger will send a bill marked "Past Due."

So why the outrage, why the dread, if the funeral is dark
As you willed it to be, and the stained glass luminous
With temporary light? Why not rest here, in the nave,

Where the living will pass by and murmur how rich
Your life was, after all, in the end? Say "I am poor,"
Show them the invisible patches in your black suit,

Ask them to praise your forgetfulness and make it last.

The Eclipses

I am a blood dot on a yolk sac, gazing out
       at a black firmament.
The sun in the form of my father's face peers in
       through a sheet of glass.
Soon he offers me roses I am meant to reject,
       being, despite myself, a boy.
When I fail his abstruse tests, he turns into
       a small mouse-gray hat.
My mother, my suffering mother,
       is caught in the revolving door
to an emergency ward. I kiss her as she spins
       until she cries, "Let me go!"
Miss Shakespeare steam-presses a label
       on my homemade poetry book.
To an unruly class of boys she reads aloud
       my *cordon-bleu* piece
about lost astronauts and a lunar eclipse.
       One of their jeering stones
undoes my senses, and I waken in the room
       of a kind mute boy
who nuzzles in my neck like a pony.
       I feed him apples and carrots,
and he grows a mane and prances round
       a makeshift corral.
At graduation I sell him to a wan Chinese boy
       in a yellow cheongsam,
who will enact the rest of my life
       as if I, not he, were the mirror.
There follows a horsy travelogue interspersed
       with erroneous zettel
on disintegrating scraps of parchment.
       Heraclitus: "What happens

to the river after you step into it?"
        Wittgenstein: "The veil that hides
the eternal reflects daylight; gaze into it,
        and the sun will blind you."
Many serving trays, typewriters, cash registers
        follow, as well as beds
covered in stray crumbs and invisible dollar bills.
        In one bed is a tall pilot
who deposits me on a tatami mat in Prague.
        A flock of cranes
demands English from me, which they suck dry
        from straws in my throat.
I stroll through the Castle with my friends, admiring
        the inexplicable pagodas
and the Pinakothek done up in Vuillard wallpapers
        like a one-size-fits-all Home,
until Mei-Mei and Guillaume hand me a cell phone
        that whispers, "Prodigal, return!"
My mother's death room is so dark I can only sense
        the sound of weeping
and the disembodied voice of my ancient father,
        who tells me to turn on the light.

Acknowledgments

Grateful acknowledgment is made to the editors of the following publications, where these poems, some in earlier versions, first appeared:

Bellevue Literary Review: "Counterprayer" and "Word";
The Georgia Review: "Tempo";
The Kenyon Review: "Synapse";
Margie/The American Journal of Poetry: "Ballad of Infinite Forgetfulness," "Black Screen," and "The Similes";
The New Yorker: "Eden," "Empty Room," "Fiber Optics," "Grandfather Writes His Will," "My Mother's Hands," "Pattern," "The Repetitions," "Salt," and "The Solitary";
The Open Boat: Poems from Asian America (edited by Garrett Hongo): "Grandfather's Rockery";
Southwest Review: "Singularities";
Witness: "My Father at 21" and "Thalia."

"Salt" was also reprinted in *Poems for the New Century* (chosen by Alice Quinn, Dana Gioia, and Rodney Phillips), and "Eden" in *Poems for America* (edited by Carmela Ciuraru) and *The Open Boat: Poems from Asian America*. The quotation from the *Bhagavad-Gita* in "The Candle" comes from the translation by Barbara Stoler Miller. The last line of "Eden" paraphrases a passage from *Gravity and Grace*, by Simone Weil. The penultimate stanza of "Asperger" paraphrases a passage from the poem "On the Paintings of Bamboo by Wen Tong," by Su Shih.

Special warm thanks to Alice Quinn.

About the Author

David Woo was born in 1959 in Phoenix, Arizona. He studied English literature at Harvard College and Stanford University, and received his M.A. in Chinese studies from Yale University. His first published poem appeared in *The New Yorker* in 1990. His work has also been published in *The Kenyon Review, The Georgia Review, Southwest Review, The Open Boat: Poems from Asian America,* and other journals and anthologies. Woo lives in Scottsdale, Arizona.

BOA Editions, Ltd.

THE A. POULIN, JR. NEW POETS OF AMERICA SERIES

Colophon

The Eclipses, poems by David Woo,
was set in Monotype Dante by Richard Foerster, York Beach, Maine.
The cover was designed by Geri McCormick, Rochester, New York.
The cover art, "Rotating Lamp" by David Woo, is courtesy of the author.
Manufacturing by McNaughton & Gunn, Ann Arbor, Michigan.

OOO

The publication of this book was made possible in part
by the special support of the following individuals:

Jan & Larry Alder OOO Alan & Nancy Cameros
Bradley P. & Debra Kang Dean
Michael & Izuru Delgado OOO Suzanne & Peter Durant
Dr. Henry & Beverly French
Dane & Judy Gordon OOO Kip & Deb Hale
William B. Hauser
Peter & Robin Hursh OOO Robert & Willy Hursh
Archie & Pat Kutz
Rosemary & Lew Lloyd OOO Patti & Barry MacNaughton
Dr. Glenn & Jennie Pang
Boo Poulin OOO Deborah Ronnen
Annette & Aaron Satloff
Ben & Joyce Tom OOO Hugh & Trudy Tom
The Lilli Tom Family
Roy Tom & Kathy Ikeda
Paul Tortorella OOO Salvatore Troia
Thomas R. Ward
Donald H. Woo, Sr.
Mr. & Mrs. Donald H. Woo, Jr. & Family
Jack & Joyce Woo OOO Thomas & Sara Woo
Elaine Yee & Jeff Emmack
Peggy & Chimey Zarotsang
The Zarotsang Family (U.S.A. & Nepal)
Pat & Michael Wilder

OOO